D1193652

COMMEMORATIVE BOTTLES

Identification & Value Guide

Bob & Debra Henrich

COLLECTOR BOOKS
A Division of Schroeder Publishing Co., Inc.

The current values in this book should be used only as a guide. They are not intended to set prices, which vary from one section of the country to another. Auction prices as well as dealer prices vary greatly and are affected by condition and demand. Neither the Authors nor the Publisher assumes responsibility for any losses which might be incurred as a result of consulting this guide.

Searching For A Publisher?

We are always looking for knowledgeable people considered experts within their fields. If you feel that there is a real need for a book on your collectible subject and have a large comprehensive collection, contant Collector Books

On the Cover

Front cover, top row, left to right:
    Walt Disney World 25th Anniversary, 8 oz., $25.00;
    Super Bowl XVIII, 10 oz., $10.00;
    Glass with Class, 10 oz., $15.00;
    World of Coca-Cola, 8 oz., $10.00.
Bottom row, left to right:
    The Fabulous Florida Keys, 8 oz., $5.00;
    Colorado Rockies Inaugural Season, 8 oz., $5.00;
    Florida Marlins, 8 oz., $5.00;
    Houston Rockets, 8 oz., $5.00.
Back cover, left to right:
    Republican National Convention, 8 oz., $50.00;
    Los Angeles XXIII Olympiad, 10 oz., $35.00;
    Super Bowl XXIX, 8 oz., $5.00;
    World of Coca-Cola, 8 oz., $10.00.

Cover Design: Beth Summers
Book Layout: Karen Geary

Collector Books
P.O. Box 3009
Paducah, KY 42002-3009

Copyright 1998 by Bob & Debra Henrich

All rights reserved. No part of this book may be reproduced, stored in any retrieval system, or transmitted in any form, or by any means including but not limited to electronic, mechanical, photocopy, recording, or otherwise, without the written consent of the authors and publisher.

Printed in the U.S.A. by Image Graphics, Paducah, KY

CONTENTS

ACKNOWLEDGMENTS

There are so many wonderful people who have contributed their time and knowledge to help us in our research. Words cannot express the appreciation that Bob and I feel.

We offer our warmest appreciation to Leonard Adams, Jeff and Brenda Cummins, Kathy and Tom Driggers, Carl Hofmann, Silvio Kimmel, Joe Morales, Ted and Ruth Oswalt, Stacha Reed, Charles Smith, Don Stephens, and many other folks on the Internet and in our travels who have extended their time to us.

The following individuals buy, sell, and trade Coca-Cola Commemorative bottles:

The Black Cat Trading Company
Joe Morales, President
1000 Ponce de Leon, Suite 100
Coral Gables, FL 33134
(305) 448-7703
e-mail: BLKCAT1000@aol.com

Don and Alexa Stephens
416 Crestmore
Mattoon, IL 61938
(217) 234-2748

Silvio Kimmel
(405) 386-3389

Jeff and Brenda Cummins
PO Box 387
Clear Creek, IN 47426
(812) 876-9076

Leonard Adams
21 S. 1st Ave.
Hartley, IA 51346
(712) 728-2550

Charles Smith
(770) 478-6523
e-mail: csmith@cyberatl.net

INTRODUCTION

I began collecting Coca-Cola memorabilia fifteen years ago, with the purchase of a 1950s Cavalier Coke machine. I started picking up bottles at antique shows and I have been hooked ever since.

Commemorative bottles hold a special appeal due to the variety of subjects which are displayed on them. Sports, festivals, anniversaries, and holidays are just some of the subjects you can find on the front of Coca-Cola commemorative bottles.

Not all events can have a bottle produced. Each individual bottler can sponsor an organization, then the idea would have to be approved by several different committees before the bottle can be produced. Some bottling plants, such as those in Florida, Georgia, Ohio, and Texas, produce many different commemorative bottles while others produce very little or none.

Some commemorative bottles can only be obtained at the event which it commemorates. These bottles usually escalate in price based on their production number and limited availability. There are many bottles which are produced in large quantities and sold nationally. An example would be the Christmas bottles or the 1996 Olympic bottles, which could be found in practically every grocery store in the United States. They tend to be very reasonable in price and can be found throughout the country.

Bottles can be found at flea markets, on the Internet, at antique shops and antique and collectible shows, and through your local Coca-Cola collector's clubs. As with any collectible, current market values are determined by the quantity, availability, and the geographic location of the bottles.

Early commemoratives, such as the Hoover Dam bottle in the 1930s, were scarcely produced until the introduction of the ACL (applied color labeling) on bottles. This process opened up a new dimension for commemorative bottles. There are now intricate pictures and a variety of colors on the Coca-Cola commemorative bottles. These bottles give us a new item to collect and a fine item to display.

I now have a quest to help other collectors put together an extensive collection of these bottles. This book should be a good start.

Robert Henrich

HOW TO USE THIS BOOK

There are two types of indexes within this book. The first is an alphabetical index, separated into 8 and 10 ounce bottles.

I have included a second index which lists bottles by graphic codes. This index is limited to 8 ounce bottles released since 1992. Not all bottles have a code and some bottles have the same codes. However, I wanted to include this index to help the beginning collector quickly locate a bottle. An example of the code index is Florida Panthers 1996 NHL Eastern Conference Champs. Below the bar code is the date 1996-3096. The 3096 is the bottler's code for the graphics on the bottle.

Example:

GLOSSARY OF TERMS

BO: Bottle only.
Tube: Specially designed tube in which the bottles were released.
Tag: A special tag which went around the neck of the bottle.
Box: Special presentation box.

Left:
Coca-Cola Grand Opening
House Party, Birmingham, AL,
$25.00.

Center:
Cola Clan National Convention,
Alexandria, MN, $85.00.

Right:
Georgia Bulldogs, National
Football Champions, $5.00.

Left:
Olympic Winter Games,
Lake Placid, NY, Alpine Skiing,
$8.00.

Center:
Olympic Winter Games,
Lake Placid, NY, Bobsledding and
Luge, $8.00.

Right:
Olympic Winter Games,
Lake Placid, NY, Figure Skating,
$8.00.

Left:
Olympic Winter Games, Lake Placid, NY, Men's Nordic Skiing, $8.00.

Center:
Olympic Winter Games, Lake Placid, NY, Men's Speed Skating, $8.00.

Right:
Olympic Winter Games, Lake Placid, NY, Nordic Skiing, $8.00.

Left:
Olympic Winter Games, Lake Placid, NY, Women's Nordic Skiing, $8.00.

Right:
Olympic Winter Games, Lake Placid, NY, Women's Speed Skating, $8.00.

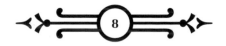

Left:
America's Junior Miss,
Mobile, AL, $350.00.

Center:
Baseball Winter Meetings,
Hollywood, FL, $125.00.

Right:
Clemson, National Football
Champions, $7.00.

Left:
Bear Bryant, Alabama Crimson
Tide (no tail scroll), $8.00.

Center:
Bear Bryant, Alabama Crimson
Tide (with tail scroll), $15.00.

Right:
Bear Bryant, Alabama Crimson
Tide (tail on elephant), $20.00.

Left:
Circleville Pumpkin Show,
75th Anniversary, Oct. 21–24,
Circleville, OH, $7.00.

Right:
Iowa Hawkeyes Big 10 Conference
Champions, Rose Bowl, $7.00.

Left:
Lady Techsters Basketball,
Ruston, LA, $20.00.

Right:
University of North Carolina
Tarheels, NCAA Basketball
Champs, 1981, $6.00.

Left:
Coke is it! Bottler Meeting, Atlanta, GA, $40.00.

Center:
Cola Clan National Convention, Nashville, TN, $15.00.

Right:
Dizzy Dean Graduate League World Series, Rossville, GA, $10.00.

Left:
Iowa Hawkeyes, Big 10 Conference Football, Peach Bowl, $7.00.

Center:
Lady Techsters, NCAA Women's Basketball Champions, $5.00.

Right:
Mud Island Opening, July 3, Memphis, TN, $7.00.

Left:
NCCAA, Division 1,
National Basketball Tournament,
Chattanooga, TN, $150.00.

Center:
Penn State Nittany Lions,
National Football Champions,
$8.00.

Right:
Sesquicentennial, 1832–1982,
Buffalo, NY, $7.00.

Left:
St. Louis Cardinals, World
Champions, error (12 hits listed in
game 1), $15.00.

Center:
St. Louis Cardinals, World
Champions, correct (17 hits listed
in game 1), $12.00.

Right:
Technical Division Meeting,
May 5–9, Saddlebrook, FL,
$120.00.

Left:
West Georgia College, NCAA
National Division III Football
Champs, $7.00.

Center:
150 Years of Heritage, 1833–1983,
Walker County, GA, $5.00.

Right:
America's Clean Community,
1st Place, Memphis, TN, $7.00.

Left:
Auburn Tigers, S.E.C. Football
Champions, Sugar Bowl, $5.00.

Center:
Baltimore Orioles,
World Champions, $5.00.

Right:
Birmingham Barons, Southern
League Baseball Champions,
$7.00.

Left:
Chattanooga Choo-Choo Centennial, 1980, The Grand Dome Room, $10.00.

Center:
Cola Clan 9th National Convention, Washington, DC, $30.00.

Right:
Forth Worth Coca-Cola Bottling Company Grand Opening, Summer 1983, $20.00.

Left:
Fred L. Lewis, 46 Years of Service, Hygeia, $5,000.00.

Center:
Gilley's in Pasadena, Houston, TX, NSDA, $45.00.

Right:
Grambling State University, Eddie Robinson, $6.00.

Left:
Illini, Big 10 Football Champions, Rose Bowl, $7.00.

Center:
Introducing Diet Coke, First Run, May 2, 1983, Louisana, $20.00.

Right:
Introducing Diet Coke, January 1983, Houston, TX, $5.00.

Left:
Kentucky Derby, 109th Run, Louisville, KY, $9.00.

Center:
Little League Baseball All Stars World Champions, East Marietta, GA, $6.00.

Right:
Mizzou Basketball, Big 8 Champions, $7.00.

Left:
North Carolina State University Wolfpack, NCAA Basketball Champions, $5.00.

Center:
Studebaker Drivers Club 19th Int'l Meet, July 18–23, 1983, $10.00.

Right:
Tampa, 80 Years of Bottling, New Plant Grand Opening, $35.00.

Left:
Tennessee Valley Authority 50th Anniversary, 1933–1983, $10.00.

Center left:
UT-Chattanooga Moccasins, Southern Conference Basketball Champions, $5.00.

Center right:
Washington Redskins, Super Bowl XVII Champions, $30.00.

Right:
Watermelon Capital of the World, 250th Anniversary, 1733–1983, Cordele, GA, $5.00.

Left:
12th Annual Million Pines Arts & Crafts Festival, Soperton, GA, $5.00.

Center:
200 Years Celebration, 1784–1984, Clarksville, TN, $10.00.

Right:
200th Anniversary, Prince Hall, Free & Accepted Masons, Winston Salem, NC, $10.00.

Left:
30th Anniversary, WDEF-TV12, Chattanooga, TN, $15.00.

Center:
America's Clean Community, 1st Place, Memphis, TN, $7.00.

Right:
Arizona State Fair, Celebration of the Century, 1884–1984, $7.00.

Left:
Big Bear, 50 Years, Quality Supermarkets Since 1934, $9.00.

Center:
Brian's Bash, Gilley's in Pasadena, TX, $30.00.

Right:
Cola Clan 10th Annual Convention, August 1–4, Sacremento, CA, $35.00.

Left:
Dallas Cowboys, Silver Season, 1960–1984, correct, $20.00.

Center:
Dallas Cowboys, Silver Season, 1960–1984, error (ties not listed), $75.00.

Right:
E.W. James & Sons Supermarkets, 50th Anniversary, 1934–1984, $6.00.

Left:
Emma Sansom High School,
Alabama State 5-A Football
Champions, $15.00.

Center:
Florida Gators, SEC Champs,
$10.00.

Right:
Georgetown University,
National Basketball Champions,
$6.00.

Left:
Georgia Tech Alumni Association,
75th Anniversary, $15.00.

Center:
Glass with Class, Federation of
Historical Bottle Clubs,
Montgomery, AL, $15.00.

Right:
Gordon Lee Trojans,
Class "A" State Baseball Champs,
$10.00.

Left:
Happy 30th Birthday, George,
$300.00.

Center:
Historic Madison, GA, The City
Sherman Refused to Burn, $5.00.

Right:
Jim Feix, The Winningest Coach in
Western Kentucky Football, $9.00.

Left:
Johnston Coca-Cola Youth Classic,
green logo, $7.00.

Center:
Kentucky Derby, 110th Run for the
Roses, Louisville, KY, $6.00.

Right:
Kentucky Heartland Festival,
August 24–26, $7.00.

Left:
Los Angeles XXIII
Olympiad, (Sam the
Eagle in dark blue),
BO, $15.00.

Center:
Los Angeles XXIII
Olympiad, (Sam the
Eagle in dark blue),
in special box and tag,
$35.00.

Right:
Los Angeles XXIII
Olympiad, (Sam the
Eagle in blue), $5.00.

Left:
Methodist Bicentennial,
1784–1984, $7.00.

Center:
National Autism Week, Honorary
Chairman, Steve Lundquist, $6.00.

Right:
Rock Eagle, World's Largest 4-H
Center, 30 Years of Service to
1,000,000 Citizens of Georgia,
1954–1984, $7.00.

Left:
Springtime in Atlanta,
"The Unforgettable Forties,"
$45.00.

Center:
Super Bowl XVIII, January 22,
Tampa, FL, $10.00.

Right:
Troy State University Trojans,
NCAA Division II Football National
Champions, $10.00.

Left:
United States Slo-Pitch Softball,
Georgia Tournament, $9.00.

Center:
Vidalia Sweet Onion Festival,
May 18–20, $6.00.

Right:
Winning Together, Coca-Cola
Bottling, Sept. 20, 1984, $40.00.

Left:
10th Annual Historic Fair,
Oct. 5 & 6, Andersonville, GA,
$6.00.

Center:
1st Annual July 4th Celebration,
Manteca, CA, $35.00.

Right:
Annie Oakley Days, 22nd Annual,
July 23–28, Greenville, OH,
$100.00.

Left:
Bank of Chickamauga 75th
Anniversary, 1910–1985, $45.00.

Center:
Bill Chappell, Over 200 Career
Victories, Dalton High School
Catamounts, $15.00.

Right:
Cherry Blossom Festival,
3rd Annual, March 17–24,
Macon, GA, $7.00.

Left:
Church of God Orphanage,
Established 1920, Cleveland, TN,
$5.00.

Center:
Coca-Cola Plant Grand Opening,
April 1985, Montgomery, AL,
$25.00.

Right:
Cola Clan, 11th Annual Convention,
The Great Texas Showdown,
Dallas, TX, $35.00.

Left:
Ethnic Festival, South Bend, IN,
$125.00.

Center:
Everett's Supermarket,
Celebrating 50 Years, Goshen, IN,
$125.00.

Right:
Exchange Club 1st Annual
Softball Tournament, Cartersville,
GA, $8.00.

Left:
Georgia Southern Eagles, National Football Champions, $8.00.

Center:
Hardees, Thanks! For 3 Great Years, 1982–1985, The Coca-Cola Company, $50.00.

Right:
Hoover Dam Golden Anniversary, 1935–1985, $80.00 BO, $125.00 with box.

Left:
Ingles 100th Store Opening, November 1985, $7.00.

Center:
Iowa Hawkeyes, Big 10 Football Champs, Freedom Bowl, $6.00.

Right:
Iowa Hawkeyes, Big 10 Football Champs, Freedom Bowl, error (colors reversed), $75.00.

Left:
Israel Expo '85 International,
March 23–31, Atlanta, GA, $6.00.

Center:
Jacksonville State University,
National Basketball Champions,
$7.00.

Right:
Jimmy Carter, 39th President of
the United States, $200.00.

Left:
Johnny Williamson Retirement,
June 30, 1985, Paris, TX, $75.00.

Center:
Johnston Coca-Cola Youth Classic
Baseball, green logo, $5.00.

Right:
Kansas City Royals, 1985 World
Champions, Show Me Series,
$12.00.

Left:
Kentuckiana 1985 Fun Summer
Weekend, 6th annual, $45.00.

Center:
MTSU Blue Raiders, 1985 OVC
Football Champions, $8.00.

Right:
New Coke Introduction,
May 6, 1985, Houston, TX, $10.00.

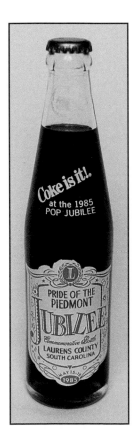

Left:
Pride of Piedmont Jubilee,
Laurens County, South Carolina,
blue logo, $8.00.

Center:
Robinson Humphrey American
Express, 90th Anniversary, $6.00.

Right:
Salvation Army International
Youth Congress, Western Illinois,
July 17–24, $60.00.

Left:
Square Dance 34th National Convention, June 27–29, 1985, Birmingham, AL, $7.00.

Center:
Star Market 70th Anniversary, 1915–1985, Boston, MA, $7.00.

Right:
State Junior & Senior League Championships, Cordele, GA, $6.00.

Left:
Tallapoosa, Georgia, 125 Years, 1860–1985, The Dogwood City, $10.00.

Center:
Tennessee State Troopers, 56 Years of Service, 1929–1985, $10.00.

Right:
Tom Mix 6th Annual National Festival, Sept. 1985, Dubois, PA, $20.00.

Left:
Ty Cobb, The Georgia Peach,
$250.00.

Center:
University of Georgia Bicentennial,
1784–1984, $5.00.

Right:
University of Georgia National
Men's Tennis Champions, $10.00.

Left:
University of Southern Mississippi
75th Anniversary, 1910–1985,
$5.00.

Center:
University of Tennessee Vols,
1985 S.E.C. Football Champions,
$12.00.

Right:
University of Tennessee Vols,
1985 Sugar Bowl Champions,
$15.00.

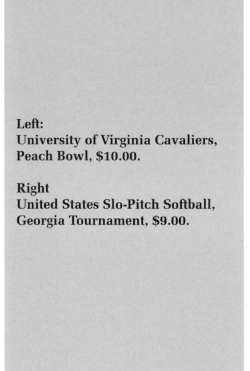

Left:
University of Virginia Cavaliers,
Peach Bowl, $10.00.

Right
United States Slo-Pitch Softball,
Georgia Tournament, $9.00.

Left:
Valdosta High School Wildcats,
State and National Football
Champs, Valdosta, GA, $5.00.

Right:
YMCA Scuba Program, 25th
Anniversary, 1960–1985, $50.00.

Left:
20th Autumn Leaf Arts & Crafts Festival, Maysville, GA, $18.00.

Center:
2nd Annual July 4th Celebration, Manteca, CA, $35.00.

Right:
4-H Kentucky Leadership Center, $7.00.

Left:
AAA State Wrestling Championship, 1986, $17.00.

Center:
Augusta's 250th Birthday Celebration, James Edward Oglethorpe, Founder of Augusta, GA, $6.00.

Right:
Banks County Holiday Festival, September 1, 1986, Homer, GA, $25.00.

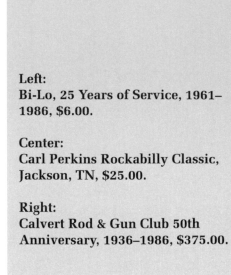

Left:
Bi-Lo, 25 Years of Service, 1961–1986, $6.00.

Center:
Carl Perkins Rockabilly Classic, Jackson, TN, $25.00.

Right:
Calvert Rod & Gun Club 50th Anniversary, 1936–1986, $375.00.

Left:
Church of God Centennial Celebration, 1886–1986, $8.00.

Center:
Coca-Cola Bottling Co. 80th Anniversary, South Bend, IN, $500.00.

Right:
Coca-Cola Collectors International 12th Annual Convention, Atlanta, GA, $30.00.

Left:
Crawford W. Long, Discoverer of Anesthesia, 175th Birthday, Madison Co., GA, $15.00.

Center:
1986 Main Street Project, Downtown Development Association, Paris, TX, $50.00.

Right:
East Tennessee State University 75th Anniversary, 1911–1986, $10.00.

Left:
Eddie Robinson, "324" Winningest Coach in College Football, Grambling State University, $10.00.

Center:
Georgia Southern Eagles, National Football Champions, $8.00.

Right:
Hart Co. Georgia AAA State Basketball Champions, error (red label), $225.00.

Left:
Hart Co. Georgia AAA State Basketball Champions, correct (orange label), $20.00.

Center:
High School AA State Football Champions, West Rome, GA, $15.00.

Right:
Iowa Hawkeyes, Big 10 Football Champions, Rose Bowl, $8.00.

Left:
Joe Frank Harris, 50th Birthday, February 16, 1986, 78th Governor of Georgia, $45.00.

Center:
Johnston Coca-Cola Youth Classic Baseball, gold logo, $7.00.

Right:
Kiwanis International, Indiana District, 70th Anniversary, 1916–1986, $30.00.

Left:
Miss Resaca Beach,
North Georgia's Gateway to the
Gulf, $60.00.

Center:
Naval Aviation 75th Anniversary,
Hygeia Coca-Cola Bottling Co.,
$10.00.

Right:
Penn State Nittany Lions
National Champions, Joe Paterno,
Undefeated Season, $10.00.

Left:
Pride of Piedmont Jubilee,
Laurens Co., South Carolina,
green logo, $7.00.

Center:
SCAMA 40th Anniversary, $65.00.

Right:
Sesquicentennial, 1836–1986,
Milford, Indiana, $350.00.

Left:
Sesquicentennial Celebration, 150th Anniversary, Brockway, PA, $200.00.

Center:
Site of the World's Largest Easter Egg Hunt, Homer, GA, $65.00.

Right:
Smitty's Supermarkets, 1961–1986, 25th Anniversary, Phoenix, AZ, $40.00.

Left:
13th Annual Snellville Days, 1974–1986, May 3–4, Snellville, GA, $10.00.

Center:
Springtime in Tennessee, Gatlinburg, TN, March 27–29, 1986, $35.00.

Right:
Tennessee Homecoming '86, 100th Anniversary, $6.00.

Left:
Tricentennial, Albany, NY,
Still Making History, 1686–1986,
$55.00.

Center:
Tyrus Raymond Cobb,
Royston Lodge 52 Remembers Ty,
$1,200.00.

Right:
United States Slo-Pitch Softball
Association Youth Classic, Dalton,
GA, $25.00.

Left:
University of Louisville, 1986
National Basketball Champions,
$6.00.

Center:
Washington Redskins Celebrating
50 Years in Washington DC,
$15.00.

Right:
Winthrop College, 100 Years,
1886–1986, $15.00.

Left:
3rd Annual July 4th Celebration, Manteca, CA, $50.00.

Center:
American Numismatic Associations 96th Convention, Atlanta, GA, $20.00.

Right:
Arizona State University, Rose Bowl and Pack 10 Football Champions, $25.00.

Left:
Atlanta Christian College, 50th Anniversary, 1937–1987, East Point, GA, $30.00.

Center:
Austin Peay State University, Ohio Valley Conference Basketball Champions, $15.00.

Right:
Centennial Celebration, 1887–1987, Community Bank and Trust, Cornelia, GA, $18.00.

Left:
Central High School Lions, 1987 State AA Football Champions, $35.00.

Center:
Coca-Cola Central Bottling, 75th Anniversary, Williamsport, PA, $18.00.

Right:
Coca-Cola Collector's Club International, 13th Annual Convention, Pete Rose, Cincinnati, OH, $95.00.

Left:
Gold Rush Days, 1987, Dahlonega Jaycees, Dahlonega, GA, $30.00.

Center:
Holly Hill, 1887–1987,
Proud Past – Progressive Future,
Holly Hill, SC, $300.00.

Right:
Johnny Lee, PERA Club Steak Fry & Street Dance, $45.00.

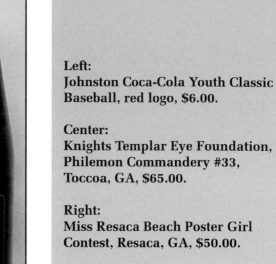

Left:
Johnston Coca-Cola Youth Classic Baseball, red logo, $6.00.

Center:
Knights Templar Eye Foundation, Philemon Commandery #33, Toccoa, GA, $65.00.

Right:
Miss Resaca Beach Poster Girl Contest, Resaca, GA, $50.00.

Left:
Northeast Louisiana University, 1987 National NCAA 1-AA Football Champions, $10.00.

Center:
6th Annual Okiefest, October 25, 1987, Tulsa, OK, $35.00.

Right:
Pride of Piedmont Jubilee, Laurens Co., SC, May 14–17, 1987, yellow logo, $6.00.

Left:
Ramesses, the Great, Exhibition, Memphis Convention Center, Memphis, TN, $7.00.

Center:
Rod Carew, Minnesota Twins Baseball, Minneapolis, MN, $45.00.

Right:
Sesquicentennial, 1836–1987, New Paris, IN, $275.00.

Left:
Sesquicentennial, 1837–1987, Syracuse, IN, $350.00.

Center:
Special Olympics, 19th Annual Area 4 Track & Field Meet, April 25, 1987, $35.00.

Right:
Springtime in Atlanta, Christmas in Dixie, April 16–18, 1987, Santa on bottle, $45.00.

Left:
Tybee Island Centennial
Celebration, 1887–1987, $5.00.

Center:
University of South Mississippi
Golden Eagles, NIT Basketball
Champions, $100.00.

Right:
Wal-Mart 25th Anniversary,
1962–1987, $30.00.

Left:
West Tennessee 50th Anniversary
Strawberry Festival, Humboldt,
TN, $5.00.

Right:
Zep 50th Anniversary, 1937–1987,
$135.00.

Left:
4th Annual July 4th Celebration, 1988, Manteca, CA, $35.00.

Center:
Bill Elliott, 1988 Winston Cup Champion, $30.00.

Right:
Cabbage Patch Kids 10th Anniversary, 1978–1988, Cleveland, GA, $115.00.

Left:
Casey Jones Village, The Old Country Store 10th Anniversary, Jackson, TN, $7.00.

Center:
Coca-Cola Bottling Company 75th Anniversary, Tarpon Springs, FL, $25.00.

Right:
Gilmer Jaycees Independence Celebration, $28.00.

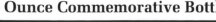

Left:
Hardees 3,000th Restaurant
Opening, March 16, 1988,
Augusta, GA, $60.00.

Center:
Hayesville High School
Lady Yellowjackets,
North Carolina State Basketball
Champions, $35.00.

Right:
JDF International, The Diabetes
Research Foundation, $30.00.

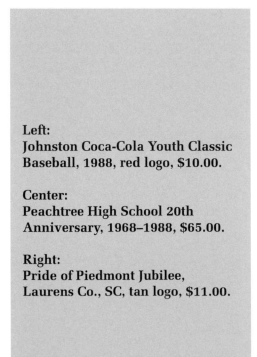

Left:
Johnston Coca-Cola Youth Classic
Baseball, 1988, red logo, $10.00.

Center:
Peachtree High School 20th
Anniversary, 1968–1988, $65.00.

Right:
Pride of Piedmont Jubilee,
Laurens Co., SC, tan logo, $11.00.

Left:
Red Food Stores 6th Annual Cancer Control Program (ACS), May 1988, $6.00.

Center:
Shriners Childrens Hospital XV, Greenville Unit, 60 Beds (Orthopaedic), Greenville, SC, $12.00.

Right:
Shriners Childrens Hospital XXIV, $12.00.

Left:
Springtime in Atlanta, A Tropical Paradise, March 31–April 2, 1988, $35.00.

Right:
Washington Redskins, Super Bowl XXII Champions, January 31, 1988, $30.00.

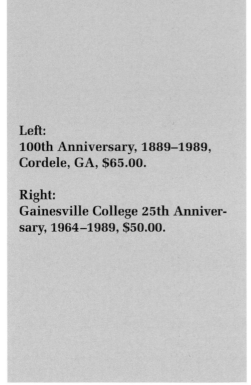

Left:
100th Anniversary, 1889–1989, Cordele, GA, $65.00.

Right:
Gainesville College 25th Anniversary, 1964–1989, $50.00.

Left:
Gold Rush Days 1989, Dahlonega Jaycees, 10th Anniversary of the Gold Dome Project, Dahlonega, GA, $35.00.

Center:
Kiwanis Club 50th Anniversary, 1939–1989, Rockmart, GA, error (Coke label on neck on back of bottle), $225.00.

Right:
Kiwanis Club 50th Anniversary, 1939–1989, Rockmart, GA, $95.00.

Left:
L.U.L.A.C. 60th Anniversary, blue logo, $225.00.

Center:
L.U.L.A.C. 60th Anniversary, white logo, $20.00.

Right:
Montana Centennial, 1889–1989, The Big Drive of '89 (wagon), $15.00.

Left:
Montana Centennial, 1889–1989, The Big Drive of '89 (steer), $15.00.

Center:
North Dakota Centennial Celebration, 1889–1989, $8.00.

Right:
North Dakota Statehood, 1889–1989, The Great Seal of the State of North Dakota, $8.00.

Left:
North Dakota Centennial, 1889–1989, Native Americans, $8.00.

Center:
Piggly Wiggly 70th Anniversary, 1919–1989, $12.00.

Right:
South Dakota, 1889–1989, Celebrate the Century of Mount Rushmore, $7.00.

Left:
Sunbelt Agricultural Exposition, Oct. 17–19, 1989, Moultrie, GA, $10.00.

Right:
Sun & Fun Florida, June 1989, Fifties Bash, $45.00.

Left:
Swain High Maroon Devils,
North Carolina State Football
Champions, $35.00.

Center:
Tanner Medical Center 40th
Anniversary, 1949–1989, $35.00.

Right:
Ty Cobb, First in the Hall of Fame,
$175.00.

Left:
Vince Dooley's Silver Anniversary
at the University of Georgia,
$45.00.

Right:
YAARAB Shrine Temple
Centennial, 1889–1989, Atlanta,
GA, $5.00.

Left:
Aurora Farmer's Fair, Indiana's Oldest Festival, Aurora Lions Club, $35.00.

Right:
Bagel Fest '90, July 28, Mattoon, IL, $30.00.

Left:
Bishop, GA Centennial, 1890–1990, Oconee County, GA, $25.00.

Center:
Chattanooga Lookouts Baseball Club, 1990 Team, $95.00.

Right:
Coca-Cola Collectors Club International 16th Annual Convention, Louisville, KY, $50.00.

Left:
Dee Dowis, 6th Place Heisman Trophy, Air Force Quarterback, $50.00.

Center:
Georgia Southern University, 1990 Division 1AA National Football Champions, $10.00.

Right:
Georgia Tech Yellow Jackets, 1990 National Football Champions, $6.00.

Left:
Indian Summer Seafood Festival, 10th Anniversary, Panama City Beach, Florida, $7.00.

Center:
Spring Jubilee, April 7–8, 1990, Historical Pendleton, SC, $25.00.

Right:
Springtime in Atlanta, Celebrating Coca-Cola...and Sports, April 12–14, 1990, $45.00.

Left:
Sunbelt Agricultural Exposition, October 18–20, 1990, Moultrie, GA, $10.00.

Center:
World of Coca-Cola, Atlanta Grand Opening, August 3, 1990, $85.00.

Right:
Museum of York County 40th Anniversary, 1950–1990, $30.00.

10 Ounce Commemorative Bottles – 1991

Left:
Aurora Farmer's Fair, Indiana's Oldest Festival, October 3–5, 1991, Aurora Lions Club, $10.00.

Center:
Broom Corn Festival, Sept 6–8, 1991, Arcola, IL, $25.00.

Right:
Coca-Cola Bottling Company, 75th Anniversary, Columbus, IN, $85.00.

Left:
Coca-Cola Collectors Club Int'l 17th Annual Convention, Scottsdale, AZ, $95.00.

Right:
Duke University, 1991 National Basketball Champions, Road to Indiana, $6.00.

Left:
Hardees, The First 30 Years, October 19, 1991, orange logo, $250.00.

Center:
Hardees, The First 30 Years, May 5, 1991, error (gold logo), $125.00.

Right:
Hardees, The First 30 Years, May 5, 1991, correct (orange logo), $150.00.

Left:
Kull's 100th Anniversary, 1891–1991, special certificate and tag, $150.00.

Right:
Opryland 20th Anniversary, $10.00.

Left:
Production Advisory Council, Tempe Production Center, $450.00.

Center:
Smoky Fest '91, May 16–18, 1991, Gatlinburg, TN, $30.00.

Right:
Springtime in Atlanta, A Great Combination, March 28–30, 1991, $30.00.

Left:
Sun N Fun Florida, June 20–22, 1991, Clearwater Beach, FL, $45.00.

Right:
Sunbelt Agricultural Exposition, Oct. 15–17, 1991, Moultrie, GA, $8.00.

Left:
Celebrating 50 Years, 1942–1992, Oak Ridge, TN, $8.00.

Center:
Coca-Cola Collectors Club Int'l, 1992 Annual Convention, Orlando, FL, $45.00.

Right:
Morehouse College 125th Anniversary, 1867–1992, $6.00.

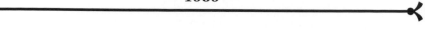

Cape Cod Coca-Cola bottles were produced for the 50th anniversary of the Cape Cod Coca-Cola bottling plant. A different bottle was produced for each of the 23 cities within the Cape Cod bottling plant distribution area. The only difference on each is the bottom of the bottle is embossed with a different city within Massachusetts.

Those Massachusetts cities are Brewster, Barnstable, Bourne, Carver, Chatham, Dennis, Eastham, Falmouth, Harwich, Kingston, Lakeville, Halifax, Mashpee, Middlesboro, Orleans, Provincetown, Plymouth, Plympton, Sandwich, Truro, Wareham, Wellfleet, and Yarmouth. $15.00 each bottle.

8 Ounce Commemorative Bottles – 1990

Left:
Christmas Bottle International, Bangladesh, $15.00.

Center:
Christmas Bottle International, Brazil, $15.00.

Right:
Christmas Bottle International, Bulgaria, $15.00.

Left:
Christmas Bottle International, China, $15.00.

Center:
Christmas Bottle International, Germany, $15.00.

Right:
Christmas Bottle International, Greece, $15.00.

Left:
Christmas Bottle International, Korea, $15.00.

Center:
Christmas Bottle International, Pakistan, $15.00.

Right:
Christmas Bottle International, Somalia, $15.00.

Left:
Christmas Bottle International, Soviet Union, $15.00.

Center:
Christmas Bottle International, Spain, $15.00.

Right:
Christmas Bottle International, Sri Lanka, $15.00.

Left:
Christmas Bottle International, Sweden, $15.00.

Center:
Christmas Bottle International, Thailand, $15.00.

Right:
Christmas Bottle International, USA, $15.00.

Left:
Bulldog Club of America
100th Anniversary, 1890–1990,
Atlanta, GA, $15.00.

Center:
Genuardi Supermarkets 70th
Anniversary, 1920–1990, $15.00.

Right:
McDonald's Owner Operator
Convention, with box, $175.00;
bottle only, $150.00.

Left:
Atlanta 1996 Olympic, Coca-Cola
Salutes Atlanta, $6.00.

Center:
City of Henderson, North Carolina,
Anniversary Celebration,
150 Years, 1841–1991, $15.00.

Right:
Domino's Pizza International
Expo '91, August 4–7, 1991,
30 Years, $125.00.

Left:
Hapeville, GA, 1891–1991, $125.00.

Right:
Hilton Conference, July 10–12, 1991, Chicago, IL, $100.00.

Left:
Holiday Inn 40th Anniversary, 1952–1992, gold logo, No Refill is clear, $275.00.

Right:
Holiday Inn 40th Anniversary, 1952–1992, yellow logo, No Refill is white, $175.00.

Left:
IGA 65th Anniversary, $75.00.

Left:
New Orleans Saints, 1991 NFC
Western Division Champions,
code #2657, $5.00.

Center:
Piggly Wiggly Diamond Jubilee,
75th Anniversary on neck, $45.00;
75th Anniversary and no refill
over Piggly Wiggly logo, $175.00.

Right:
Alan C. Pope High School
Greyhounds, $15.00.

Left:
Season's Greeting, Santa Claus, $5.00.

Right:
Season's Greeting, Santa Claus (with 5 cents refund), $5.00.

Left:
Silver Dollar City, Missouri, 1891–1991, Branson, MO, embossed on base plate, $8.00.

Center:
Southwest Airlines, 20 Years of Loving You!, $75.00.

Right:
Shaw AFB, 50 Years, Pride of Summer, 1941–1991, $15.00.

Left:
75th Anniversary, 1917–1992, Richmond, IN, $15.00.

Center:
150th Anniversary, 1842–1992, Fort Smith, AR, $10.00.

Right:
AA Food Services 30th Anniversary, #1 in Northwest Georgia, code #2471, $45.00.

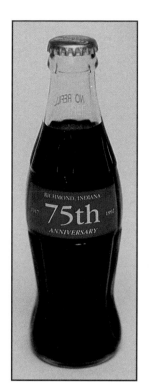

Left:
Albertville Olympics, $5.00.

Right:
Almacs 50th Anniversary, $10.00.

Left:
Barcelona Olympics, Refund 5 cents, states listed, $5.00.

Center:
Barcelona Olympics, No Refill, $5.00.

Right:
CAA, Creative Artist Agency, Inc., $125.00.

Left:
Carrollton, GA, Fire Dept., $25.00.

Center:
Coca-Cola, Fifth Avenue, NY, red and gray logo, $15.00.

Right:
Congressional Hispanic Caucus Institute, Inc., Edward R. Roybal, $650.00.

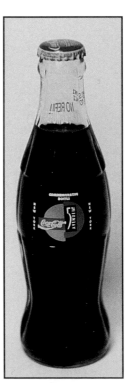

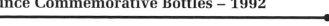

Left:
Crawford W. Long, Discovered Anesthesia 1842, Jefferson, GA, $20.00.

Center:
Eckerd, 40 Years of Caring for You!, '52 – '92, $275.00.

Right:
Fiesta Texas, "Come Celebrate the Spirit of Texas," May 1992, San Antonio, TX, $15.00.

Left:
Harrison High School Hoyas, $12.00.

Center:
Holiday Inn Crowne Plaza, A World of Difference, $350.00.

Right:
Hot August Nights, Reno (no car displayed), $25.00.

Left:
K-Mart 30th Anniversary,
1962–1992, $200.00.

Center:
Minyard Food Stores, 60 Years,
1932–1992, $75.00.

Right:
Person County Bicentennial,
200 Years of Progress, 1792–1992,
$10.00.

Left:
Phar-Mor, 10 Years, $350.00.

Center:
Re/Max, #1 in Georgia, 10th Year,
$25.00.

Right:
Republican National Convention
Gala 1992, Houston, Texas,
$450.00.

Left:
Rite Aid, The Leader For Over 30 Years, 1962–1992, $250.00.

Center:
Rome Jaycees, Celebrating 50 years of service to our community, $30.00.

Right:
St. Louis Cardinals 100th Anniversary, 1892–1992, $5.00.

Left:
Springtime in Atlanta, The Springtime Express, April 15–18, 1992, $45.00.

Right:
SuperValu 50th Anniversary, 1942–1992, $75.00 BO; $100.00 with box.

Left:
Sunbelt Agricultural Exposition, 15th Anniversary, Moultrie, GA, code #3431, $10.00.

Center:
Tall Ships 1992, Newport, RI, $15.00.

Right:
The Treaty of Greene Ville, Fort Greene Ville, OH, $40.00.

Left:
Tony Jones, Cleveland Browns Salutes, Royston, GA, code #3181, $30.00.

Center:
University of Alabama, National Champions, "Century of Champions," 1892–1992, code #4464, $5.00.

Right:
Warner Robins High School Demons, Robert Davis 200 Career Victories, $35.00.

Left:
World of Coca-Cola 1st Anniversary (Coke on the neck), $15.00.

Center:
World of Coca-Cola 2nd Anniversary, August 3, 1992, $25.00.

Right:
World of Coca-Cola 2nd Anniversary, error (date missing), $18.00.

8 Ounce Commemorative Bottles – 1993

Left:
90th Anniversary, Fort Smith, AR, code #2434, $5.00.

Center:
American Airlines, CR Smith Museum, $350.00.

Right:
ARA Partnership Profitability, $300.00.

Left:
Babyland General Hospital 15th Anniversary, Cabbage Patch, Cleveland, GA, code #2819, $45.00.

Center:
Baltimore Orioles, 1993 All-Star Game, July 13, 1993, Oriole Park at Camden Yards, code #917, $5.00.

Right:
Baylor School, Chattanooga, TN, 1893–1993, $5.00.

Left:
Best of the Bay, San Franciso 49ers, code #391, $5.00.

Center:
Best of the Bay, Oakland Athletics, code #389, $5.00.

Right:
Best of the Bay, San Fransico Giants, code #390, $5.00.

Left:
Best of the Bay, Oakland Raiders, code #392, $5.00.

Center:
Best of the Bay, San Jose Sharks, code #484, $5.00.

Right:
Best of the Bay, Golden State Warriors, code #393, $5.00.

Left:
Blimpie Annual Franchise Convention, Atlanta, GA, $50.00 with tag.

Center:
Boise River Festival, code #1449, $10.00.

Right:
Business Planning Meeting, Coca-Cola USA Creative Service, $500.00.

Left:
Byerly's 25, A Tradition of Style, code #118, $5.00.

Center:
CM Tanner Grocery Co. 100th Birthday, 1893–1993, June 17, 1993, code #2561, $25.00.

Right:
Canton Super Bowl Kickoff II, January 1993, Pro Football Hall of Fame, Canton, OH, code #3953, $150.00.

Left:
Carolina Panthers, October 26, 1993, code #5106, $5.00.

Center:
Casey's General Store 25th Anniversary, 1968–1993, $225.00.

Right:
Charles P. Taylor, Grand Commander, Knights Templar of Georgia, May 1993, $200.00.

Left:
Cherokee Strip, Relive the Legend, 1893–1993, 100th Anniversary, code #2158, $15.00.

Center:
Cheyenne Frontier Days, 97th Annual, July 23–August 1, 1993, code #1412, $5.00.

Right:
Circle City Classic, 10th Anniversary, October 2, 1993, Indianapolis Hoosier Dome, code #1678, $60.00.

Left:
Colorado Rockies Inaugural Season, code #3948, $5.00.

Center:
Colorado Rockies, MLB 1993 Record Season Attendance, Don Baylor, code #5777, $5.00.

Right:
Colorado Rockies, 1993 MLB Record Season Attendance, Jerry McMorris, code #5777, $5.00.

Left:
Coca-Cola Collectors Club
19th Annual Convention,
Dearborn, MI, $30.00.

Center:
Cub Foods 25th Anniversary,
1968–1993, code #3248, $150.00.

Right:
Dallas Cowboys, Super Bowl XXVII
Champions, code #207, $5.00.

Left:
Deer Lodge, Hiawassee, GA,
code #3608, $35.00.

Center:
Denver Broncos, First Team Logo,
code #3446, $5.00.

Right:
Dunwoody Wildcats, 1993 AAAA
Georgia State Champions, $25.00.

Left:
Federal Prison Retirees
Association 30th Anniversary,
1963–1993, $75.00.

Center:
Florida Panthers, NHL Hockey
Team Inaugural Season, code
#2873, $5.00.

Right:
Florida State University, 1993
National Football Champions,
code #95, $5.00.

Left:
Git-N-Go 35th Anniversary, Since
1958, code #3510, $5.00.

Center:
Graceland, Memphis, TN,
code #2308, $5.00.

Right:
Grand Canyon Railway, Est. 1901,
code #2157, $10.00.

Left:
Happy Holidays, Marietta College Park Productions, $300.00.

Center:
Kiwanis Club of Jonesboro, GA, Home of *Gone with the Wind*, code #2560, $40.00.

Right:
Hot August Nights, Reno, code #1417, $20.00.

Hot August Nights, three bottle set with presentation box and letter, Corvette, code #1745; Thunderbird, code #1746; Chevy, code #1747; $100.00; BO $10.00.

Left:
LSU Tigers, National Baseball Champions, code #3187, $5.00.

Center:
Marlins Inaugural Season, code #4142, $5.00.

Right:
McDonough Cougars Football, $20.00.

Left:
NBA All-Star Weekend, February 19–21, 1993, Salt Lake City, UT, code #4007, $15.00.

Right:
NCAA Final Four, New Orleans, set with pins and coins, code #91, $15.00; BO $5.00.

Left:
NCLR 25th Anniversary National Convention, July 18–22, 1993, code #2798, $350.00.

Right:
National Restaurant Association Restaurant, Hotel, and Motel Show, $350.00.

Left:
NHIS, New Hampshire International Speedway, Inaugural Winston Cup 500, code #967, $10.00.

Center:
Northwestern High Trojans, Division 1 AAAA State Football Champions, $20.00.

Right:
Ohio State Buckeyes 25th Anniversary, 1968 National Football Champions, code #4575, $5.00.

Left:
Rodgers & Hammerstein's
Oklahoma!, Celebrating 50 Years,
code #3357, $5.00.

Center:
Okmulgee Pecan Festival, 10th
Anniversary, code #1987, $5.00.

Right:
Pat Summit, Celebrating 20 Seasons
of Success, Lady Volunteers,
code #3819, $5.00.

Left:
Phoenix Suns, 25th Anniversary,
code #222, $10.00.

Center:
Phoenix Suns, Western Conference
Champions, Alvin Adams, code
#4565, $5.00.

Right:
Phoenix Suns, Western Conference
Champions, Connie Hawkins,
code #4568, $5.00.

Left:
Phoenix Suns, Western Conference Champions, Dick Van Arsdale, code #4569, $5.00.

Center:
Phoenix Suns, Western Conference Champions, Paul Westphal, code #4567, $5.00.

Right:
Pilot Club of Carrollton, GA, 48 Years of Service, 1945–1993, $90.00.

Left:
Production Advisory Council, $250.00.

Center:
6th Ronald McDonald House Show, Frank & Son Trucking, code #3746, $75.00.

Right:
Rossville Bank 30th Anniversary, 1963–1993, code #5094, $50.00.

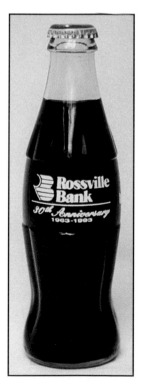

Left:
Sam Houston Bicentennial
Birthday Celebration, code #710,
$5.00.

Center:
San Diego Padres Baseball Club,
25 Years, 1969–1993, code #93,
$10.00.

Right:
Season's Greetings, December
1993, code #3576, $5.00.

Left:
SmokyFest, May 13–15, 1993,
Gatlinburg, TN, $35.00.

Center:
Springtime in Atlanta, Everything
is coming up Springtime, code
#845, $25.00.

Right:
Sunbelt Agricultural Exposition,
Inc. 16th Anniversary, Moultrie,
GA, code #1546, $5.00.

Left:
Sun & Fun 1993, The Beauties, Clearwater Beach, FL, code #618, $45.00.

Right:
Telluride Limited Edition, 1993–1994, code #3525, $10.00.

Left:
Tennessee Aquarium, Chattanooga, TN, $10.00.

Center:
Texas Tech Lady Raiders, NCAA Champions, code #1647, $5.00.

Right:
U.S. Olympic Festival '93, San Antonio, TX, code #1877, $5.00.

Left:
University of Maine Black Bears, NCAA Division I Ice Hockey Champions, code #1844, $5.00.

Center:
University of North Alabama, The Perfect Season, Division II National Football Champions, code #62, $5.00.

Right:
Wayne County High School, Region Champions, code #595, $45.00.

Left:
The World of Coca-Cola, Always Coke Classic, $15.00.

Right:
The World of Coca-Cola, 3rd Anniversary, $20.00.

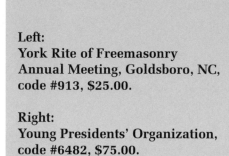

Left:
York Rite of Freemasonry Annual Meeting, Goldsboro, NC, code #913, $25.00.

Right:
Young Presidents' Organization, code #6482, $75.00.

8 Ounce Commemorative Bottles – 1994

Left:
200 Years of Fort Defiance, Ohio, 1794–1994, code #1761, $10.00.

Center:
AFL-AFC Kansas City Chiefs 35th Anniversary, code #3406, $5.00.

Right:
Agnes Scott College, code #3964, $50.00.

Left:
Arkansas Razorbacks Football,
100 Years, 1894–1994, code #2835,
$5.00.

Center:
Arkansas Razorbacks, 1994
National Basketball Champs, code
#2893, $5.00.

Right:
Atlanta Knights, Turner Cup
Champions, code #4799, $20.00.

Left:
Azalea Festival, Honor Heights
Park, Muskogee, OK, code
#6141, $5.00.

Right:
7th Annual Badger Spring Pause,
Spring Round Up, May 13–14,
1994, Wisconsin Dells, WI, Travel
Refreshed, $125.00.

Left:
Ballpark in Arlington, Est. 1994, code #870, $5.00.

Center:
Basket Village U.S.A., code #2987, $5.00.

Right:
Biedenharn, 100 Years, 1894–1994, Vicksburg, MI, code #5115, $5.00.

Left:
Boise River Festival '94, code #1086, $5.00.

Center:
Brickyard 400 Indianapolis Motor Speedway, code #2637, $95.00.

Right:
Caribbean Refrescos, Inc., 25th Anniversario, 1969–1994, code #4220, $350.00.

Left:
Charles P. Taylor, 120th Grand Commander Knights Temple, May 12, 1994, $75.00.

Center:
98th Annual Cheyenne Frontier Days, July 23–31, 1994, code #2330, $5.00.

Right:
Choo Choo Chapter, 10th Anniversary Picnic, October 22, 1994, $85.00.

Left:
Choo Choo Connection, August 11–13, 1994, $75.00.

Center:
Cincinnati Reds First Season, National League Central Division, code #2576, $5.00.

Right:
Cincinnati Reds, World Champions 1919, 1940, 1975, 1976, 1990, code #2575, $5.00.

Left:
Cleveland Cavaliers vs Rockets, code #3637, $5.00.

Center:
Cobb County Humane Society, code #5096, $95.00.

Right:
Coca-Cola Fifth Avenue, NY, gray and gold logo, code #2704, $15.00.

Left:
Coca-Cola Collectors Club 20th National Convention, Atlanta, GA, $45.00.

Center:
D.W. Brooks, Founder of Gold Kist, Royston Hall of Fame, code #3654, $40.00.

Right:
Detroit Lions Football, Year of the Fan, code #3656, $5.00.

Left:
Dallas Cowboys, Super Bowl
XXVIII Champions, code #6228,
$5.00.

Center:
Denny's Franchise Convention,
$250.00.

Right:
DollyWood Heartsong, code #1014,
$5.00.

Left:
Final Draw, 1994 FIFA WorldCup,
code #4576, $250.00.

Center:
Flagstaff, AZ, Centennial,
1894–1994, code #1938, $5.00.

Right:
Florida Marlins 1994, code #966,
$5.00.

Left:
Golden Eagle Basketball, code #4961, $50.00.

Center:
Grand Canyon Railway, code #4306, $5.00.

Right:
Great Get Together, Coca-Cola Collectors Club, Buena Park, CA, $60.00.

Left:
Guam's 50th Liberation Day, Golden Salute, code #894, $10.00.

Center:
Happy Holidays with Santa, code #3699, $5.00; with tube $15.00.

Right:
Historic Natchez, a classic on the Mississippi, code #667, $5.00.

Left:
Holiday Greetings, Wal-Mart embossed on bottom of bottle, $5.00.

Right:
Hot August Nights, August 3–7, 1994, Reno, code #2345, $10.00.

Left:
Hot August Nights, '56 blue Chevy, code #2734, $5.00.

Right:
Hot August Nights, three bottle set in box with letter, $50.00.

Left:
Hot August Nights, Woody wagon, code #2733, $5.00.

Center:
Hot August Nights, red Plymouth DeSoto convertible, code #2735, $5.00.

Right:
Houston Livestock Show and Rodeo, code #5177, $5.00.

Left:
Houston Rockets, NBA World Champions 1994, code #3293, $5.00.

Center:
Huck's 20th Anniversary, code #2677, $5.00.

Right:
Johnny Mize, "The Big Cat," Hall of Fame 1981, Royston, GA, code #4271, $50.00.

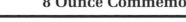

Left:
Junior League of Fort Smith, AR, Holiday Market, Nov. 3–5, 1994, code #4474, $50.00.

Center:
Kennesaw State Fighting Owls, 1994 NAIA Baseball National Champions, code #4978, $15.00.

Right:
Lazy "E" Arena 10th Anniversary, code #2837, $5.00.

Left:
Lee Christian School, Founded 1994, Sanford, NC, code #4234, $35.00.

Center:
Lenox Square 35th Anniversary, 1959–1994, code #2788, $30.00.

Right:
Mardi Gras 1994, New Orleans, LA, code #5406, $5.00.

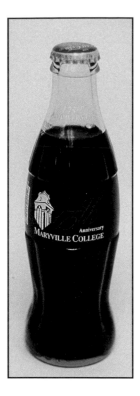

Left:
Maryville College 175th Anniversary, code #2352, $5.00.

Center:
McDonald's 1st Drive-In, Oklahoma City, code #2347, $15.00.

Right:
McDonald's Ronald McDonald House, RMCC, June 10, 1994, Atlanta, GA, $50.00.

Left:
McDonald's Ronald McDonald House, RMCC, Oct. 15, 1994, Chicago, IL, code #4257, $95.00.

Center:
Merry Christmas, College Park & Marietta Production, code #4765, $250.00.

Right:
Mickey's Toontown, Disneyland, Anaheim, CA, code #1330, $20.00.

Left:
Milwaukee Brewers 25th Anniversary, 1970–1994, code #1973, $5.00.

Center:
Minnefest '94 Convention, 20th Anniversary, Minnesota 1st Chapter, 1974–1994, C.C.C.C., $125.00.

Right:
NBA All-Star Weekend, Minnesota, Feb. 11–13, 1994, code #4104, $5.00.

Left:
NCAA Final Four, Charlotte, NC, April 1–4, 1994, code #4282, $5.00.

Center:
Nahunta Volunteer Fire Department, Celebrating 35 Years of Service to the Nahunta Community, Wayne County, NC, code #864, $100.00.

Right:
National Finals Rodeo, XXXVI, Las Vegas, code #3408, $5.00.

Left:
New Orleans Jazz & Heritage Festival, 25th Anniversary, code #213, $5.00.

Center:
Northeastern State University, 1994 NAIA Football Champs, code #1963, $5.00.

Right:
Ohio Winterfest, 11th Anniversary, Zanesville, OH, $125.00.

Left:
Peachtree Road Race 25th Anniversary, Atlanta Track Club, code #1822, $5.00.

Center:
Portland Trailblazers 25th Anniversary, code #102, $5.00.

Right:
Portland Trailblazers, NBA Franchise Granted Feb. 6, 1970, code #94, $5.00.

Left:
Portland Trailblazers, 1977 NBA Champs, code #93, $5.00.

Center:
Portland Trailblazers, Clyde Drexler, code #97, $5.00.

Right:
Portland Trailblazers, Geoff Petrie, code #96, $5.00.

Left:
Portland Trailblazers, Bill Walton, code #98, $5.00.

Center:
Reno Rodeo, Celebrating 75 Years, code #1092, $5.00.

Right:
Rossville Lodge #397 F. & A.M. 100th Anniversary, 1894–1994, code #3944, $30.00.

Left:
Sacramento Kings Basketball, May 22, 1994, code #1387, $5.00.

Center:
Coca-Cola Bottling Co. Inc. of Santa Fe 75th Anniversary, code #3810, $5.00.

Right:
Selena, 5 Anos Contigo…, Celebrando Tejano 1994, code #3603, $50.00.

Left:
Shiloh National Military Park 100th Anniversary, 1894–1994, code #2344, with box $25.00; BO $15.00.

Right:
Ski-Hi Stampede, Colorado's Oldest Pro Rodeo, Monte Vista, CO, code #940, $5.00.

Left:
Smoky Fest 1994, May 19–21, Gatlinburg, TN, $40.00.

Center:
South Metro Employees, Happy Holidays, with polar bear, code 4977, $200.00.

Right:
Space Center, Houston, Celebration 25, Man on the Moon, July 20, 1969, code #2507, $5.00.

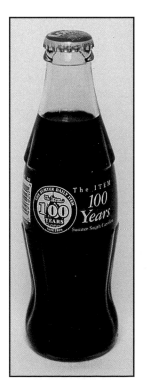

Left:
Sumter Daily Item, 100 Years, Sumter, SC, code #2645, $5.00.

Center:
Sunbelt AG Exposition, Oct. 18–20, 1994, Moultrie, GA, code #2504, $5.00.

Right:
Super Bowl II, Packers vs Raiders, Orange Bowl, January 14, 1968, code #3283, $5.00.

Left:
Super Bowl III, Jets vs Colts, Orange Bowl, January 12, 1969, code #3390, $5.00.

Center:
Super Bowl V, Colts vs Cowboys, Orange Bowl, January 17, 1971, code #3391, $5.00.

Right:
Super Bowl X, Steelers vs Cowboys, Orange Bowl, January 18, 1976, code #3392, $5.00.

Left:
Super Bowl XIII, Steelers vs Cowboys, Orange Bowl, January 21, 1979, code #3293, $5.00.

Right:
Super Bowl XXIII, 49ers vs Bengals, Orange Bowl, January 22, 1989, code #3394, $5.00.

Super Bowl XXVIII, Georgia
Dome, January 30, 1994, code
#6228, BO $5.00; pin/box $75.00.

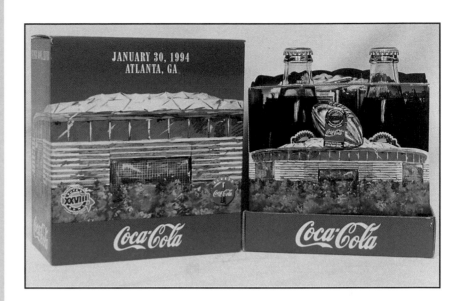

Left:
Telephone Pioneers of America,
code #4522, $85.00.

Center:
Telluride, 1994–1995, $5.00.

Left:
Time Saver 40th Anniversary,
1954–1994, code #948, $5.00.

Left:
Thigpen Pharmacy, 10 Years of Caring, blue logo, Pikeville, NC, code #5096, $70.00.

Center:
Thigpen Pharmacy, 10 Years of Caring, red logo, Pikeville, NC, code #5096, $150.00.

Right:
Tulsa, OK, Zoo Polar Care '94, Build the Bear Necessities, code #3265, $5.00.

Left:
Ty Cobb, The Georgia Peach, code #3298, $100.00.

Center:
Township of Springfield, Union County, NJ, Bicentennial Celebration, 1794–1994, $10.00.

Right:
University of Kentucky Wildcats Basketball, blue logo, code #4654, $5.00.

Left:
The University of Tennessee, Celebrating 200 Years of Learning, 1794–1994, code #4078, $5.00.

Center:
University of Vermont Catamounts, code #104, $5.00.

Right:
U.S. Olympic Festival '94, St. Louis Gateway to the Gold, code #1453, $5.00.

Left:
Utah Jazz, 1994, code #177, $5.00.

Center:
ValuJet, Our First Birthday, Oct. 26, 1994, code #3104, $70.00.

Right:
Walton High School Raiders, National School of Excellence, code #3817, $25.00.

Left:
Warehouse Markets Since 1938, code #2346, $5.00.

Center:
Wendy's Franchise Restaurants, 25 Years of Quality, code #3595, two bottle set in box, $400.00; BO $95.00.

Right:
WorldCup Soccer USA 94, Argentina's flag, code #5527, $5.00.

Left:
WorldCup Soccer USA 94, Brazil's flag, code #5523, $5.00.

Center:
WorldCup Soccer USA 94, Germany's flag, code #5528, $5.00.

Right:
WorldCup Soccer USA 94, Italy's flag, code #4582, $5.00.

Left:
WorldCup Soccer USA 94,
Mexico's flag, code #5522, $5.00.

Center:
WorldCup Soccer USA 94,
USA's flag, code #5532, $5.00.

Right:
WorldCup Soccer USA 94,
host city Boston, MA, code #4525,
$5.00.

Left:
WorldCup Soccer USA 94, host
city Chicago, IL, code #4688,
$5.00.

Center:
WorldCup Soccer USA 94,
host city Dallas, TX, code #4650,
$5.00.

Right:
WorldCup Soccer USA 94,
host city Detroit, MI, code #4644,
$5.00.

Left:
WorldCup Soccer USA 94, host city Los Angeles, CA, code #4643, $5.00.

Center:
WorldCup Soccer USA 94, host cities New York/New Jersey, code #4652, $5.00.

Right:
WorldCup Soccer USA 94, host city Orlando, FL, code #4686, $5.00.

Left:
WorldCup Soccer USA 94, host city San Francisco, CA, code #4687, $5.00.

Right:
WorldCup Soccer USA 94, host city Washington, DC, code #4689, $5.00.

Left:
WorldCup Soccer USA 94 special colorful tube containing pin and WorldCup Soccer USA 94 bottle, $15.00.

Right:
The World of Coca-Cola 4th Anniversary, Atlanta, GA, $15.00.

Left:
The World of Coca-Cola, Atlanta, GA, with The World of Coca-Cola on neck, $5.00.

Center:
YMCA 150th World Anniversary, code #946, $5.00.

Right:
Young Brothers Pharmacy, First Painted Wall Sign, Cartersville, GA, code #6482, $40.00.

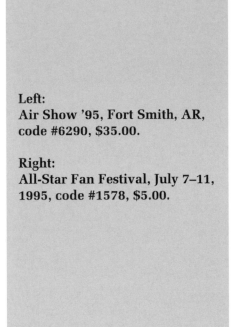

Left:
Air Show '95, Fort Smith, AR, code #6290, $35.00.

Right:
All-Star Fan Festival, July 7–11, 1995, code #1578, $5.00.

Left:
Astrodome 30th Anniversary, code #149, $5.00.

Center:
Atlanta Braves, 1995 World Champions, code #214, $5.00.

Right:
Atlanta Falcons 30th Anniversary, code #2136, $10.00.

Left:
Atlanta Olympics (first of six),
One Year To Go, code #639, $5.00.

Center:
Atlanta Olympics (second of six),
From Athens to Atlanta,
Celebrating 100 Years of Olympic
Tradition, code #2170, $5.00.

Right:
Azalea Festival, Honor Heights
Park, Muskogee, OK, code #409,
$5.00.

Left:
Badger Chapter 8th Annual
Spring Pause, Let's watch for 'em,
code #1541, $125.00.

Center:
Ballet Oklahoma, Since 1972,
Bryan Pitts, Artistic Director, code
#5009, $5.00.

Right:
Baskin Robbins 50th Anniversary,
code #871, $250.00.

Left:
Boise River Festival, June 22–25, 1995, code #1051, $5.00.

Center:
Cal Ripken Jr., 1995 The Record Breaking Year, code #2726, $5.00.

Right:
California State Fair, Aug. 18– Sept. 4, 1995, code #2036, $5.00.

Left:
Canton Super Bowl Kick Off IV, January 1995, code #4900, $125.00.

Right:
99th Annual Cheyenne Frontier Days, July 21–30, 1995, code #406, $5.00.

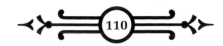

Left:
Christmas 1995, employee bottle, Santa at fireplace with note, $250.00.

Center:
Christmas 1995, Santa in green chair, code #2433, $5.00.

Right:
Christmas 1995, Santa saying "Shhh!" to barking dog, code #2432, $5.00.

Left:
Christmas 1995, Santa with blonde girl, code #2431, $5.00.

Center:
Christmas 1995, Santa looking in refrigerator, code #2391, $5.00.

Right:
Cincinnati Reds logo 1869, code #534, $5.00.

Left:
Cincinnati Reds logo 1907, code #534, $5.00.

Center:
Cincinnati Reds logo 1911, code #534, $5.00.

Right:
Cincinnati Reds logo 1939, code #534, $5.00.

Left:
Cincinnati Reds logo 1995, code #534, $5.00.

Center:
Coca-Cola Collectors Club 21st Convention, Kansas City, MO, code #2363, $50.00.

Right:
Days Inn Celebrating 25 Years, code #1468, $175.00.

Left:
DollyWood, Juke Box Junction, 1995, code #1111, $5.00.

Center:
Easter Seal Society of Virginia, Celebrating Fifty Years of Service, code #1099, $45.00.

Right:
Eddie Robinson, 400th Win, Grambling State University, code #3844, $5.00.

Left:
Edward Waters College Celebrating 130 Years of Educational Excellence, code #2303, $5.00.

Center:
Emmitt Smith 1995 Season Record (Dallas Cowboy), code #89, $5.00.

Right:
Eskimo Joe's 20th Anniversary, Stillwater, OK, code #2186, $5.00.

Left:
Florida Aquarium, 1995 Inaugural Year, code #4648, $5.00.

Center:
Florida Forest Festival 1995, Perry, FL, code #1257, $75.00.

Right:
Fort Worth Stock Show Centennial, Celebrating 100 Years of Heroes, code #2831, $5.00.

Left:
Frankenmuth, 150 Years, Michigan's Little Bavaria, Founded 1845, code #1095, $5.00.

Center:
Graceland, Memphis, TN, code #1255, $8.00.

Right:
H.G. Hill Food Stores, 100 Years, Nashville Owned & Operated, code #2566, $175.00.

Left:
HWI, 50 Years, Building America since 1945, code #2138, $300.00.

Center:
Homestead Motorsports Complex, Jiffy Lube 300, November 5, 1995, Homestead, FL, code #2724, $5.00.

Right:
Hot August Nights (musical notes), Reno, code #943, $5.00.

Left:
Hot August Nights (Ford Fairlane), Reno, code #938, $5.00.

Right:
Hot August Nights, two bottle set with glass and letter in box, code #938, 943, $50.00.

Left:
Houston Livestock Show and Rodeo, code #4398, $5.00.

Center:
Houston Rockets, NBA World Champions, Back to Back 1994 & 1995, code #2236, $5.00.

Right:
Jacksonville Jaguars Inaugural Season, Sept. 3, 1995, code #2085, $5.00.

Left:
Jacksonville Jaguars logo, Jan. 20, 1995, code #1066, $5.00.

Center:
Jacksonville Jaguars, 30th NFL Franchise, code #1988, $5.00.

Right:
Jacksonville Jaguars, AFC Central Division, Nov. 2, 1994, code #4802, $5.00.

Left:
Jeff Gordon, Time to Refuel, code #2492, $5.00.

Center:
Jeff Gordon, 1995 Winston Cup Champion, code #4224, $5.00.

Right:
Kentucky Derby, 121st Running, Louisville, KY, code #4684, $5.00.

Left:
Kroger Grand Opening, Savannah Historical District, The Best of the Old and New, code #1542, $350.00.

Center:
Lewiston, Maine, Bicentennial, 1795–1995, code #1113, $5.00.

Right:
Long John Silvers/Coca-Cola, Always Working Together, code #4553, $175.00.

Left:
Mardi Gras 1995, New Orleans, code #4570, $5.00.

Center:
Marine Hotel, Catering & Duty Free Association Conference & Trade Show, 10th Anniversary, April 30–May 3, 1995, Naples, FL, code #986, $175.00.

Right:
McDonald's & Coca-Cola, Partners 40 Years, $175.00.

Left:
McDonald's Ronald McDonald House, Hawaii, $75.00.

Center:
McEachern High School Indians, Powder Springs, GA, code #4792, $25.00.

Right:
Merry Christmas 1995, College Park & Marietta Production, BO $200.00; three bottle set, $450.00.

Left:
NATO/ShoWest, 100 Years of
Movie Magic, code #499, $100.00.

Center:
NBA All-Star Weekend, Phoenix,
AZ, code #3534, $5.00.

Right:
NCAA Final Four Basketball,
Seattle, WA, code #3975, $5.00.

Left:
NFL Exhibition Game, Knoxville,
TN, August 12, 1995, code #2172,
$5.00.

Center:
National Finals Rodeo, Las Vegas,
NV, code #2442, $5.00.

Right:
National Gymnastics Championships, New Orleans, LA, code
#1597, $5.00.

Left:
Nebraska Football Champions,
Go Big Red, code #2033, $5.00.

Center:
North Metro Sales Center, Happy
Holidays 1995, $175.00.

Right:
Northern Indiana First Parade
circus bottle, code #2161, $45.00.

Left:
Norwich Navigators, code #105,
$5.00.

Center:
OSU Heisman Trophy Winner
1974, Archie Griffin, code #1361,
$5.00.

Right:
OSU Heisman Trophy Winner
1975, Archie Griffin, code #1362,
$5.00.

Left:
OSU Heisman Trophy Winner 1955, Howard "Hopalong" Cassady, code #1360, $5.00.

Center:
OSU Heisman Trophy Winner 1944, Les Horvath, code #1357, $5.00.

Right:
OSU Heisman Trophy Winner 1950, Vic Janowicz, code #1358, $5.00.

Left:
OSU Heisman Trophy, 5 Winners, code #1359, $5.00.

Right:
Ohio Winterfest 1995, Zanesville, OH, code #3957, two bottle set, $250.00.

Left:
Omaha Zoo, code #1093, $5.00.

Center:
Purgatory Resort 30th Anniversary, Durango, CO, code #2395, $5.00.

Right:
Rotary Club of Clearwater, FL, International President Herb Brown, $30.00.

Left:
San Francisco 49ers, Five Time Super Bowl Champions, code #5188, $5.00.

Center:
Showeast, Atlantic City, NJ, code #3126, $175.00.

Right:
South Metro, Happy Holidays 1995, $175.00.

Left:
St. Louis Rams Inaugural Season, code #2544, $5.00.

Center:
Stanford Law School, code #2966, $175.00.

Right:
Star Market 80th Anniversary, 1915–1995, code #1429, $15.00.

Left:
Sunbelt Agricultural Exposition, Moultrie, GA, code #1821, $5.00.

Center:
Super Bowl XXIX, Joe Robbie Stadium, code #3395, BO $5.00; box, bottle & pin, $20.00.

Right:
TAMACC (Texas Association of Mexican-American Chamber of Commerce), Championing Hispanic Business, code #1938, $95.00.

Left:
Tall Stacks '95, October 11–15, code #1991, $5.00.

Center:
Tennessee Tech, 25 Years of Golden Eaglette Basketball, code #4215, $5.00.

Right:
Toast to Disney & Ovitz from Coca-Cola, Oct. 3, 1995, $550.00.

Left:
Ty Cobb, Baseball's Best, Birthplace, Banks County, code #1377, $75.00.

Center:
Waffle House 40th Anniversary, 1955–1995, America's Place to Eat, code #3003, $250.00.

Right:
World of Coca-Cola 5th Anniversary, Aug. 3, 1995, $10.00.

There is much discussion on the next two bottles regarding their legitimacy. We have included them and hope to have further updates in our next book.

Left:
David Letterman, Our Beverage Buddy, June 1995, $500.00.

Right:
President's Club, MCI Sales and Service Operations, wording etched on neck, $3,000.00.

Left:
AFDO Association of Food & Drug Officials, Founded in 1896, $100.00.

Center:
Analyst-Portfolio Managers Meeting, March 11–12, 1996, $250.00.

Right:
Atlanta 1996 Olympics, Official Olympic Escort Runner, The 1996 Olympic Torch Relay, $175.00.

Left:
Atlanta 1996 Olympics, Official Olympic Torchbearer, $175.00.

Center:
Atlanta 1996 Olympics, Olympic Torch Relay, Bringing the Flame to Atlanta, 3rd in set of 6, code #23, $5.00.

Right:
Atlanta 1996 Olympics, Centennial Olympic Stadium, 5th in set of 6, code #1163, $5.00.

Left:
Atlanta 1996 Olympics, Refreshing the Olympic Spirit, 4th in set of 6, code #63, $5.00; error (green torch reversed), $25.00.

Right:
Atlanta 1996 Olympics, Atlanta Welcomes the World, 6th in set of 6, code #1317, $5.00.

Left:
Atlanta 1996 Olympic Torch
Relay, code #49, $5.00.

Center:
Atlanta 1996 Olympic Torch
Relay, Dallas/Fort Worth, TX,
code #192, $5.00.

Right:
Atlanta 1996 Olympic Torch
Relay, Houston, TX, code #199,
$5.00.

Left:
Atlanta 1996 Olympic Torch
Relay, New Orleans, LA, code
#191, $5.00.

Center:
Atlanta 1996 Olympic City,
Athletics, Atlanta, GA, $15.00.

Right:
Atlanta 1996 Olympic City,
Baseball, Atlanta, GA, $15.00.

Left:
Atlanta 1996 Olympic City, Basketball, Atlanta, GA, $15.00.

Center:
Atlanta 1996 Olympic City, Cycling, Atlanta, GA, $15.00.

Right:
Atlanta 1996 Olympic City, Gymnastics, Atlanta, GA, $15.00.

Left:
Atlanta 1996 Olympic City, Musee Olympique Lausanne, Atlanta, GA, $15.00.

Center:
Atlanta 1996 Olympic City, For the Fans, Atlanta, GA, $15.00.

Right:
Atlanta 1996 Olympic, Coca-Cola Olympic Pin Trading Center, $25.00.

Left:
Atlanta 1996 Olympics, Olympic Host Bottler, yellow torch, $125.00; error (Dynamic Ribbon, gold torch), $150.00.

Right:
Atlanta Syrup Branch, Coca-Cola USA Fountain, 110th Anniversary, $150.00.

Left:
Azalea Festival, Honor Heights Park, Muskogee, OK, code #4512, $5.00.

Center:
Badger Chapter, 9th Annual Badger Spring Pause, code #1344, $75.00.

Right:
Baltimore Ravens Inaugural Season 1996, code #2429, $5.00.

Left:
Bemidji, Celebrating Our Centennial, First City on the Mississippi, code #1352, $5.00.

Center:
The First Annual Global Beverage Package Design Conference, $150.00.

Right:
Big E Celebrating 75 Years, West Springfield, MA, code #2381, $5.00.

Left:
Boise River Festival, code #1129, $5.00.

Center:
California State Fair, code #1518, $5.00.

Right:
Capitol Revival, Columbus, OH, code #559, $5.00.

Left:
Canon Greater Hartford Open, June 24–30, 1996, 45 Years, code #538, $5.00.

Center:
Carolina Panthers Inaugural Season at Ericsson Stadium, code #1175, $5.00.

Right:
100th Annual Cheyenne Frontier Days, code #542, $5.00.

Left:
Chick-Fil-A Celebrating Fifty Years of Excellence in Food Services, S. Truett Cathey, Founder, code #478, $15.00.

Center:
Christmas 1996, Santa saying "Shhh!" to dog, code #1630, $5.00.

Right:
Christmas 1996, Santa in green chair, code #1631, $5.00.

Left:
Christmas 1996, Santa with boy looking in refrigerator, code #1632, $5.00.

Center:
Christmas 1996, Santa with toy train set, code #1633, $5.00.

Right:
Cincinnati Reds, Big Red Machine, World Champions, 20th Anniversary, code #2020, $5.00.

Left:
Cobb County Humane Society, $40.00.

Center:
Coca-Cola Collectors Club 22nd Convention, July 10–13, 1996, Reston, VA, $35.00.

Right:
Coca-Cola Enterprises Safe Driver Truck Roadeo, New Orleans Superdome, $150.00.

Left:
Coca-Cola Enterprises 10th Anniversary, $50.00.

Center:
Coke New York, "Drive profitable per-capita & share growth through teamwork, innovation, superior execution and a relentless pursuit of excellance," code #3519, $250.00.

Right:
College Park & Marietta Production, Happy Holidays 1996, $150.00 with box and can; $75.00 BO.

Left:
Dallas Cowboys, Super Bowl Champs 1972, 1978, 1993, 1994, 1996, code #2434, $5.00.

Center:
Dallas Cowboys, Super Bowl VI Champs, 1972, code #2434, $5.00.

Right:
Dallas Cowboys, Super Bowl XII Champs, 1978, code #2434, $5.00.

Left:
Dallas Cowboys, Super Bowl XXVII Champs, 1993, code #2434, $5.00.

Center:
Dallas Cowboys, Super Bowl XXVIII Champs, 1994, code #2434, $5.00.

Right:
Dallas Cowboys, Super Bowl XXX Champs, 1996, code #2434, $5.00.

Left:
Dare to Care, Spread a Little Sunshine, code #2201, $5.00.

Center:
Detroit Red Wings 70th Anniversary, code #3197, $5.00.

Right:
Dollywood Boulevard 1996, 11th Anniversary, code #4091, $5.00.

Left:
Doral Ryder Open 35th Anniversary, code #3550, $5.00.

Center:
Ernst & Young LLP, Entrepreneur of the Year Institute, 10th Anniversary, Palm Springs, CA, code #3689, $25.00.

Right:
Florida Panthers, 1996 NHL Eastern Conference Champions, code #3096, $5.00.

Left:
Food Distributers International, Celebrating 90 Years, $225.00.

Center:
Fort Bend County Fair & Rodeo, 60 Years, code #1748, $5.00.

Right:
George C. Snyder Day, Janary 30, 1996, $350.00.

Left:
Hardee's Commitment!, 35th Anniversary Celebration, March 31–April 2, 1996, Orlando, FL, $100.00.

Center:
Heavener Indian Territory Centennial, Oklahoma, Seal of the Choctaw Nation, code #2288, $5.00.

Right:
Historic A.C.L. Depot, San Antonio, FL, $35.00.

Left:
Homespun Festival 1996, Polk County Chamber of Commerce, code #2404, $35.00.

Center:
Hot August Nights, Reno '96, panel truck, code #1127, $5.00.

Right:
Hot August Nights 10th Anniversary, Reno '96, code #1259, $5.00.

Left:
Houston Livestock Show & Rodeo, code #4505, $5.00.

Center:
IGA 70th Anniversary, 1996 Olympic Women's Softball Gold Medal, clear bottle on logo, $100.00.

Right:
IGA 70th Anniversary, 1996 Olympic Women's Softball Gold Medal, white bottle on logo, $150.00.

Left:
Iowa Sesquicentennial, code #2313, $5.00.

Center:
Jacksonville Jaguars Inaugural Year, $5.00.

Right:
John H. Johnson, Ebony, 1945–1995, 50 Years That Changed America, $300.00.

Left:
Judge Issac C. Parker, Celebrating 100 Years of Law & Order, Ft. Smith, AR, code #2031, $5.00.

Center:
Kansas State Fair, September Magic, code #2157, $5.00.

Right:
Keeneland, 1936–1996, Lexington, KY, code #1735, $5.00.

Left:
Kennesaw State College, 1995 NCAA Softball National Champions, code #3343, $10.00.

Center:
Kentucky Derby, 122nd Running, May 4, 1996, code #198, $5.00.

Right:
LSU Tigers, 1991, 1993 & 1996 National Baseball Champions, code #2755, $5.00.

Left:
LSU Tigers, Women's Outdoor Track & Field National Champions, code #2756, $5.00.

Center:
Mardi Gras 1996, New Orleans, code #3206, $5.00.

Right:
McDonald's Ronald McDonald House Charities, October 12, 1996, code #3317, $100.00.

Left:
McDonald's Ronald McDonald House, Hawaii, code #1805, $50.00.

Center:
Miami Centennial '96, code #706, $5.00.

Right:
Michigan State University Spartan Football, 100 Seasons, code #2146, $5.00.

Left:
New Orleans Saints, 30 Seasons, code #2273, $5.00.

Center:
North Metro Coca-Cola Enterprises, Happy Holidays, $150.00.

Right:
Piedmont College, Celebrating 100 Years, $50.00.

Left:
Pro Football Hall of Fame Festival, Canton, OH, July 27, 1996, code #1569, $5.00.

Center:
QA 2000, Technical Business Conference, code #1084, $195.00.

Right:
Republican National Convention, San Diego, CA, code #1391, $50.00.

Left:
Royal Cup Coffee, "Savor the Experience," $85.00.

Center:
Salute to Excellence, 10th Anniversary, code #1673, $275.00.

Right:
Selena Funds Benefitting the Selena Foundation, XVI Tejano Music Awards, code #4554, $5.00.

Left:
Shorter College, BSBA119, $500.00.

Right:
Southwest Airlines, 25 Years of Luv, code #212, $75.00.

Left:
South Metro, Happy Holidays 1996, $150.00.

Center:
St. Louis Cardinals, 1996 Central Division Champions, code #3865, $5.00.

Right:
St. Patrick's Festival, Dublin/ Laurens, code #1407, $10.00.

Left:
Sunbelt Agricultural Exposition, Moultrie, GA, October 15–17, 1996, code #2096, $5.00.

Center:
Super Bowl XXX, January 28, 1996, Sun Devil Stadium, Tempe, AZ, code #2985, $5.00.

Right:
SYS-TAO, Great Plains, OK, code #1675, $250.00.

Left:
Sydney 2000 Olympics, Team Millennium Partner, $350.00.

Right:
Toyota Gator Bowl, 50th Anniversary, January 1, 1996, code #4262, $5.00.

Left:
Trigg County Ham Festival, code #2238, $5.00.

Center:
University of Kentucky, Always Jammin, code #3491, $5.00.

Right:
University of Kentucky, National Basketball Champions 1996, code #2018, $5.00.

Left:
University of Nebraska Football, National Back to Back Champions, '95 & '96, recalled (should have read '94 & '95), code #2407, $75.00.

Center:
University of Tennessee, 75 Years of UT Football, code #2238, $5.00.

Right:
Utility Purchasing Management Group, Dallas, TX, October 6–8, 1996, $175.00.

Left:
ValuJet MD-95 Launch, $195.00.

Center:
W. S. Heath, 1936–1996, 60 Years, Carolina Coca-Cola, Sumter, South Carolina, $400.00.

Right:
Waffle House & Coca-Cola, Partners since 1955, $275.00.

Left:
Walt Disney World 25th Anniversary, Cinderella's coach, 1 in a
series of 4, code #2710, $5.00.

Right:
Walt Disney World 25th Anniversary, Cinderella's coach, employee
bottle in tube, $25.00.

Left:
White Castle 75th Anniversary,
code #1223, in tube $175.00;
BO $95.00.

Right:
Westin Hotels & Resorts, Puerto
Rico, $250.00.

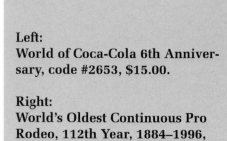

Left:
World of Coca-Cola 6th Anniversary, code #2653, $15.00.

Right:
World's Oldest Continuous Pro Rodeo, 112th Year, 1884–1996, Payson, AZ, code #1132, $5.00.

8 Ounce Commemorative Bottles – 1997

Left:
Alley Theater 50th Anniversary 1947–1997, code #2748, $5.00.

Center:
AutoZone 9th Gathering, Nashville, A New Partnership May 19, 1997, with tube $275.00; BO $250.00.

Right:
Boise River Festival, June 26–29, 1997, code #34, $5.00.

Left:
Buddy Holly Music Festival, September 4–7, 1997, Lubbock, TX, BO $5.00; with box $30.00.

Right:
Chattanooga Mocs, What a Sweet Season Basketball, code #1523, $5.00.

Left:
Chattanooga, TN, World's First Bottler of Coca-Cola, $25.00.

Center:
Coca-Cola Collectors Club 23rd Annual Convention, Colorado Springs, Smokey the Bear, $35.00.

Right:
Corinth 90th Anniversary, June 14, 1997, $35.00.

Left:
Canton, OH, Pro Football Hall of Fame Festival, July 26, 1997, code #1581, $5.00.

Center:
DollyWood 12th Anniversary, Tennessee's Place for Fun, code #1229, $5.00.

Right:
Easter Seal Society of VA, Inc., A Society of Caring Friends, $45.00.

Left:
Evander Holyfield, 3 Times Heavyweight Champion, recalled, code #4702, $10.00.

Center:
Florida Gators, 1996 National Football Champions, code #1433, $5.00.

Right:
The Fabulous Florida Keys, Conch Republic 15th Anniversary, code #2781, $5.00.

Left:
Florida State Football 50 Years, 1947–1997 Seminoles, Garnet & Golden, code #2044, $5.00.

Center:
Graceland 15th Anniversary, Elvis, Still Rockin'!, code #4333, $10.00.

Right:
Grand Canyon Railway, Since 1901, code #1034, $5.00.

Left:
Grant's Farm, St. Louis, MO, code #1307, $10.00.

Right:
Great American Cookie Company, Orlando, Fl., April 12, 1997, with tube $275.00.

Left:
Grandma's Marathon, Duluth, MN, June 1997, code #1172, $10.00.

Center:
Greenwood Round-up Club 50th Anniversary, 1947–1997, Greenwood, AR, code #4385, $5.00.

Right:
Hot August Nights, code #1435, $5.00.

20th Annual Homespun Festival, July 11–12, 1997, Rockmart, GA, BO $20.00; with tag/tube $35.00.

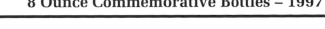

Left:
Houston Livestock Show and Rodeo, code #3918, $5.00.

Center:
Jackie Robinson, Dodgers 50th Anniversary, code #4211, $5.00.

Right:
Jackie Robinson, 50th Anniversary, code #1789, $5.00.

Left:
John Smoltz, 1996 Cy Young Award Winner, code #1410, $5.00.

Center:
123rd Kentucky Derby, May 3, 1997, code #44, $5.00.

Right:
Lady Volunteers, National Champions, code #3916, $5.00.

Left:
Martha's Vineyard, code #1259, $5.00.

Center:
Nantucket, code #1416, $5.00.

Right:
National Sheriff's Association Annual Convention & Exposition, June 22–25, 1997, Atlanta, GA, code #1523, $150.00.

Left:
NHL All-Star Weekend, San Jose, CA, June 17–18, 1997, code #3421, $5.00.

Center:
Paramount's Kings Island 25th Anniversary, code #221, $5.00.

Right:
Parke County Covered Bridge Festival, October 10–19, 1997, code #1512, $5.00.

Left:
Phoenix Coyotes Inaugural Season, code #2979, $5.00.

Center:
Rockford Speedway, 50 Years, code #1166, $5.00.

Right:
Shenandoah Apple Blossom Festival 70th Anniversary, April 30 – May 4, 1997, Winchester, Virginia, code #568, $5.00.

Left:
50th Strawberry Festival, Stillwell, OK, Centennial, code #58, $5.00.

Center:
Sunbelt Agricultural Exposition 20th Anniversary, Moultrie, GA, October 14–16, 1997, code #1309, $5.00.

Right:
Super Bowl XXXI, New Orleans, LA, Superdome, January 26, 1997, code #3477, $5.00.

Left:
Tejano Music Awards XVII, code #4123, $5.00.

Center:
Texas Motor Speedway, Coca-Cola 300 Inaugural Race, April 6, 1997, code #4399, $5.00.

Right:
Texas Rangers, 1996 West Division Champions, code #201, $5.00.

Left:
Turner Field Inaugural Season, Home of the Braves, code #484, $5.00.

Right:
University of Kentucky Wildcats, 1978 National Basketball Champions, code #34, $5.00.

Left:
Walt Disney World 25th Anniversary, Magic Kingdom Park, Since October 1, 1971, 2nd in series of 4, code #2711, $5.00.

Center:
Walt Disney World 25th Anniversary, Epcot, Since October 1, 1982, 3rd in series of 4, code #2712, $5.00.

Right:
Walt Disney World 25th Anniversary, The Disney Studios, Since May 1, 1989, 4th in series of 4, code #2713, $5.00.

Left:
World of Coca-Cola, Atlanta, code #2653, $10.00.

Center:
World of Coca-Cola, Las Vegas, code #2652, $15.00.

Right:
Zephyrs Field, 1997 Inaugural Season, code #506, $5.00.

10 OUNCE INDEX

8 OUNCE INDEX

INDEX BY CODE

COLLECTOR BOOKS
Informing Today's Collector

DOLLS, FIGURES & TEDDY BEARS

2079	**Barbie** Doll Fashion, Volume I, Eames	$24.95
3957	**Barbie** Exclusives, Rana	$18.95
4557	**Barbie,** The First 30 Years, Deutsch	$24.95
3310	**Black Dolls,** Book I, Perkins	$17.95
3810	**Chatty Cathy** Dolls, Lewis	$15.95
4559	Collectible **Action Figures,** 2nd Ed., Manos	$17.95
1529	Collector's Encyclopedia of **Barbie** Dolls, DeWein/Ashabraner	$19.95
2211	Collector's Encyclopedia of **Madame Alexander Dolls,** 1965-1990, Smith	$24.95
4863	Collector's Encyclopedia of **Vogue Dolls,** Stover/Izen	$29.95
3728	Collector's Guide to Miniature **Teddy Bears,** Powell	$17.95
4861	Collector's Guide to **Tammy,** Sabulis/Weglewski	$18.95
3967	Collector's Guide to **Trolls,** Peterson	$19.95
1799	**Effanbee Dolls,** Smith	$19.95
4571	**Liddle Kiddles,** Langford	$18.95
3826	Story of **Barbie,** Westenhouser	$19.95
1513	**Teddy Bears & Steiff** Animals, Mandel	$9.95
1817	**Teddy Bears & Steiff** Animals, 2nd Series, Mandel	$19.95
2084	**Teddy Bears, Annalee's & Steiff** Animals, 3rd Series, Mandel	$19.95
1808	Wonder of **Barbie,** Manos	$9.95
1430	World of **Barbie** Dolls, Manos	$9.95
4880	World of **Raggedy Ann Collectibles,** Avery	$24.95

TOYS, MARBLES & CHRISTMAS COLLECTIBLES

3427	**Advertising Character** Collectibles, Dotz	$17.95
2333	Antique & Collectible **Marbles,** 3rd Ed., Grist	$9.95
3827	Antique & Collector's **Toys,** 1870–1950, Longest	$24.95
3956	Baby Boomer **Games,** Identification & Value Guide, Polizzi	$24.95
4934	**Breyer Animal** Collector's Guide, Identification and Values, Browell	$19.95
1514	Character **Toys** & Collectibles, Longest	$19.95
1750	Character **Toys** & Collector's, 2nd Series, Longest	$19.95
3717	**Christmas** Collectibles, 2nd Edition, Whitmyer	$24.95
4976	**Christmas** Ornaments, Lights & Decorations, Johnson	$24.95
4737	**Christmas** Ornaments, Lights & Decorations, Vol. II, Johnson	$24.95
4739	**Christmas** Ornaments, Lights & Decorations, Vol. III, Johnson	$24.95
3874	Collectible Coca-Cola Toy **Trucks,** deCourtivron	$24.95
4849	Collectible American **Yo-Yos,** Cook	$16.95
2338	Collector's Encyclopedia of **Disneyana,** Longest, Stern	$24.95
4958	Collector's Guide to **Battery Toys,** Hultzman	$19.95
4639	Collector's Guide to **Diecast Toys** & Scale Models, Johnson	$19.95
4566	Collector's Guide to **Tootsietoys, 2nd Ed,** Richter	$19.95
3436	Grist's Big Book of **Marbles**	$19.95
3970	Grist's Machine-Made & Contemporary **Marbles,** 2nd Ed.	$9.95
4723	**Matchbox** Toys, 2nd Ed., 1947 to 1996, Johnson	$18.95
4871	**McDonald's Collectibles,** Henriques/DuVall	$19.95
1540	**Modern Toys** 1930–1980, Baker	$19.95
3888	**Motorcycle** Toys, Antique & Contemporary, Gentry/Downs	$18.95
4953	Schroeder's Collectible **Toys,** Antique to Modern Price Guide, 4th Ed	$17.95
1886	Stern's Guide to **Disney** Collectibles	$14.95
2139	Stern's Guide to **Disney** Collectibles, 2nd Series	$14.95
3975	Stern's Guide to **Disney** Collectibles, 3rd Series	$18.95
2028	**Toys,** Antique & Collectible, Longest	$14.95

JEWELRY, HATPINS, WATCHES & PURSES

1712	Antique & Collectible **Thimbles** & Accessories, Mathis	$19.95
1748	Antique **Purses,** Revised Second Ed., Holiner	$19.95
1278	Art Nouveau & Art Deco **Jewelry,** Baker	$9.95
4850	Collectible **Costume Jewelry,** Simonds	$24.95
3875	Collecting Antique **Stickpins,** Kerins	$16.95
3722	Collector's Ency. of **Compacts, Carryalls & Face Powder Boxes,** Mueller	$24.95
4940	**Costume Jewelry,** A Practical Handbook & Value Guide, Rezazadeh	$24.95
1716	Fifty Years of Collectible **Fashion Jewelry,** 1925-1975, Baker	$19.95
1424	**Hatpins** & Hatpin Holders, Baker	$9.95
1181	100 Years of Collectible **Jewelry,** 1850-1950, Baker	$9.95
2348	20th Century Fashionable Plastic **Jewelry,** Baker	$19.95
3830	Vintage **Vanity Bags & Purses,** Gerson	$24.95

FURNITURE

1457	American **Oak** Furniture, McNerney	$9.95
3716	American **Oak** Furniture, Book II, McNerney	$12.95
1118	Antique **Oak** Furniture, Hill	$7.95
2132	Collector's Encyclopedia of **American** Furniture, Vol. I, Swedberg	$24.95
2271	Collector's Encyclopedia of **American** Furniture, Vol. II, Swedberg	$24.95
3720	Collector's Encyclopedia of **American** Furniture, Vol. III, Swedberg	$24.95
3878	Collector's Guide to **Oak** Furniture, George	$12.95

1755	Furniture of the **Depression Era,** Swedberg	$19.95
3906	**Heywood-Wakefield** Modern Furniture, Rouland	$18.95
1885	**Victorian** Furniture, Our American Heritage, McNerney	$9.95
3829	**Victorian** Furniture, Our American Heritage, Book II, McNerney	$9.95

INDIANS, GUNS, KNIVES, TOOLS, PRIMITIVES

1868	Antique **Tools,** Our American Heritage, McNerney	$9.95
1426	**Arrowheads** & Projectile Points, Hothem	$7.95
2279	**Indian** Artifacts of the Midwest, Hothem	$14.95
3885	**Indian** Artifacts of the Midwest, Book II, Hothem	$16.95
1964	**Indian** Axes & Related Stone Artifacts, Hothem	$14.95
2023	**Keen Kutter** Collectibles, Heuring	$14.95
4724	Modern **Guns,** Identification & Values, 11th Ed., Quertermous	$12.95
2164	**Primitives,** Our American Heritage, McNerney	$9.95
1759	**Primitives,** Our American Heritage, Series II, McNerney	$14.95
4730	Standard **Knife** Collector's Guide, 3rd Ed., Ritchie & Stewart	$12.95

PAPER COLLECTIBLES & BOOKS

4633	**Big Little Books,** A Collector's Reference & Value Guide, Jacobs	$18.95
4710	Collector's Guide to **Children's Books,** 1850 to 1950, Jones	$18.95
1441	Collector's Guide to **Post Cards,** Wood	$9.95
2081	Guide to Collecting **Cookbooks,** Allen	$14.95
2080	Price Guide to **Cookbooks & Recipe Leaflets,** Dickinson	$9.95
3973	**Sheet Music** Reference & Price Guide, 2nd Ed., Pafik & Guiheen	$19.95
4654	**Victorian Trade Cards,** Historical Reference & Value Guide, Cheadle	$19.95
4733	**Whitman Juvenile Books,** Brown	$17.95

OTHER COLLECTIBLES

2269	Antique **Brass & Copper** Collectibles, Gaston	$16.95
1880	Antique **Iron,** McNerney	$9.95
3872	Antique **Tins,** Dodge	$24.95
4845	Antique **Typewriters** & Office Collectibles, Rehr	$19.95
1714	**Black** Collectibles, Gibbs	$19.95
1128	**Bottle** Pricing Guide, 3rd Ed., Cleveland	$7.95
3718	Collectible **Aluminum,** Grist	$16.95
4560	Collectible **Cats,** An Identification & Value Guide, Book II, Fyke	$19.95
4852	Collectible **Compact Disc** Price Guide 2, Cooper	$17.95
1634	Collector's Ency. of Figural & Novelty **Salt & Pepper Shakers,** Davern	$19.95
2020	Collector's Ency. of Figural & Novelty **Salt & Pepper Shakers,** Vol. II, Davern	$19.95
2018	Collector's Encyclopedia of **Granite Ware,** Greguire	$24.95
3430	Collector's Encyclopedia of **Granite Ware,** Book II, Greguire	$24.95
3879	Collector's Guide to Antique **Radios,** 3rd Ed., Bunis	$18.95
1916	Collector's Guide to **Art Deco,** Gaston	$14.95
4933	Collector's Guide to **Bookends,** Identification & Values, Kuritzky	$19.95
3880	Collector's Guide to **Cigarette Lighters,** Flanagan	$17.95
4887	Collector's Guide to **Creek Chub Lures** & Collectibles, Smith	$24.95
3966	Collector's Guide to **Inkwells,** Identification & Values, Badders	$18.95
3881	Collector's Guide to **Novelty Radios,** Bunis/Breed	$18.95
3730	Collector's Guide to **Transistor Radios,** Bunis	$15.95
4864	Collector's Guide to **Wallace Nutting Pictures,** Ivankovich	$18.95
1629	**Doorstops,** Identification & Values, Bertoia	$9.95
4717	**Figural Nodders,** Includes Bobbin' Heads and Swayers, Irtz	$19.95
3968	**Fishing Lure** Collectibles, Murphy/Edmisten	$24.95
4867	**Flea Market Trader,** 11th Ed., Huxford	$9.95
4944	**Flue Covers,** Collector's Value Guide, Meckley	$12.95
4945	**G-Men and FBI Toys,** Whitworth	$18.95
3819	**General Store Collectibles,** Wilson	$24.95
2215	Goldstein's **Coca-Cola** Collectibles	$16.95
4721	Huxford's Collector's **Advertising,** 3rd Ed.	$24.95
2216	**Kitchen Antiques,** 1790–1940, McNerney	$14.95
4950	The **Lone Ranger,** Collector's Reference & Value Guide, Felbinger	$18.95
2026	**Railroad** Collectibles, 4th Ed., Baker	$14.95
1632	**Salt & Pepper Shakers,** Guarnaccia	$9.95
1888	**Salt & Pepper Shakers** II, Guarnaccia	$14.95
2220	**Salt & Pepper Shakers** III, Guarnaccia	$14.95
3443	**Salt & Pepper Shakers** IV, Guarnaccia	$18.95
2096	**Silverplated Flatware,** Revised 4th Edition, Hagan	$14.95
1922	Standard **Old Bottle** Price Guide, Sellari	$14.95
3892	**Toy & Miniature Sewing Machines,** Thomas	$18.95
3828	Value Guide to **Advertising Memorabilia,** Summers	$18.95
3977	Value Guide to **Gas Station** Memorabilia, Summers	$24.95
4877	Vintage **Bar Ware,** Visakay	$24.95
4935	The W.F. Cody **Buffalo Bill** Collector's Guide with Values, Wojtowicz	$24.95
4879	**Wanted to Buy,** 6th Edition	$9.95

This is only a partial listing of the books on collectibles that are available from Collector Books. All books are well illustrated and contain current values. Most of our books are available from your local bookseller, antique dealer, or public library. If you are unable to locate certain titles in your area, you may order by mail from COLLECTOR BOOKS, P.O. Box 3009, Paducah, KY 42002-3009. Customers with Visa, MasterCard, or Discover may phone in orders from 7:00–5:00 CST, Monday–Friday, Toll Free 1-800-626-5420. Add $2.00 for postage for the first book ordered and $0.30 for each additional book. Include item number, title, and price when ordering. Allow 14 to 21 days for delivery.

Schroeder's ANTIQUES Price Guide

. . . is the #1 best-selling antiques & collectibles value guide on the market today, and here's why . . .

Schroeder's ANTIQUES Price Guide

OUR #1 BEST SELLER!

Identification & Values Of Over 50,000 Antiques & Collectibles

8½ x 11, 608 Pages, $12.95

- *More than 450 advisors, well-known dealers, and top-notch collectors work together with our editors to bring you accurate information regarding pricing and identification.*

- *More than 45,000 items in almost 550 categories are listed along with hundreds of sharp original photos that illustrate not only the rare and unusual, but the common, popular collectibles as well.*

- *Each large close-up shot shows important details clearly. Every subject is represented with histories and background information, a feature not found in any of our competitors' publications.*

- *Our editors keep abreast of newly developing trends, often adding several new categories a year as the need arises.*

If it merits the interest of today's collector, you'll find it in *Schroeder's*. And you can feel confident that the information we publish is up to date and accurate. Our advisors thoroughly check each category to spot inconsistencies, listings that may not be entirely reflective of market dealings, and lines too vague to be of merit. Only the best of the lot remains for publication.

Without doubt, you'll find
SCHROEDER'S ANTIQUES PRICE GUIDE
the only one to buy for
reliable information and values.

COLLECTOR BOOKS
A Division of Schroeder Publishing Co., Inc.